T5-DHE-487

APPLE
SAMPLER

A Collection of Fresh Apple Recipes

by Jan Siegrist

THE NEW ENGLAND PRESS, INC.

©1986 by Jan Siegrist
Second Printing, October 1986
ALL RIGHTS RESERVED

For additional copies write to:
　　The New England Press
　　P.O. Box 575
　　Shelburne, Vermont 05482

Also available: Maple Sampler
　　　　　　　　Strawberry Sampler
　　　　　　　　Zucchini Sampler

Written and illustrated by
Jan Seygal Siegrist

ISBN 0-933050-38-0

PRINTED IN THE UNITED STATES OF AMERICA

CONTENTS

Desserts

Breads, Muffins, and Rolls

And Furthermore

INTRODUCTION

The <u>APPLE</u>. This versatile fruit is simple to pick, convenient to eat, easy to store, available year-round, low in calories, and rich in pectin, an excellent source of dietary fiber. What more could you want from a fruit? From the crisp, sweet Red Delicious to the firm, tart Stayman, an apple variety exists to please every palate.

<u>Picking</u>. Although apples are available year-round, supplies are best during the fall and winter. When you harvest, be sure to pick the apple with its stem intact. When the stem is removed, a break in the skin is left which allows bacteria to enter and cause rot. When buying or picking apples, choose firm, brightly colored fruits, free from disease or insects.

<u>Storing</u>. Many apple varieties keep

well in long-term storage without processing. Winesap, York Imperial, Northern Spy, and Rome Beauty varieties will normally keep for 4-6 months. Jonathan, McIntosh, Cortland, and Delicious varieties can be stored for shorter periods. The location, seasonal conditions, maturity at picking, and length of time between picking and storing will influence the keeping quality. Careful handling to prevent bruising is essentia

Apples are best stored in a cold, well-ventilated area or in the refrigerator. A temperature around 32°F with 85-90 percent humidity is preferred for most varieties. Constant air circulation around the apples is essential to remove the gase that apples release as they ripen. Allowing these gases to build up can speed the ripening process further. Wooden boxes are ideal storage units, as are pails, baskets, and barrels. Layer packing material, such as dry leaves, crumpled burlap, or shredded paper, alternately with the apples. For short-term storage and smaller quantities, a perforated, moisture-proof bag in the refrigerator is sufficient.

 Freezing. Apples can be frozen packed dry or in a syrup. One pound of apples yields approximately 1 pint of frozen slices.

For the dry-pack method, peel, core, and slice the apples. For each pint of fruit, combine 2-4 tablespoons of sugar or honey with 2 tablespoons of lemon juice. Pour over the apples and mix well. Tightly pack the slices in heavy plastic bags or plastic freezer containers. Seal, label, and freeze.

For the syrup-pack method, dissolve $1\frac{3}{4}$ cups of sugar in 2 cups of warm water. Chill thoroughly before using. Just before packing, add $1\frac{1}{2}$ teaspoons of lemon juice (to prevent browning) to the cold syrup. Allow $\frac{1}{3}-\frac{1}{2}$ cup of syrup and about 1½ cups of fruit for each pint container. To prepare the apples, peel, core, and slice the fruit. I recommend steam blanching to preserve the nutritiona value as well as the texture of the apple. To steam blanch, place the apple slices in a wire basket suspended above 2-3 inches of boiling water in a large kettle. Cover. Begin timing for blanching when the steam starts to escape from under the lid. Blanch for 3 minutes. Remove the basket from the heat and immediately plunge the apples into cold water. Drain the cooled fruit and pack into freezer containers. Cover the slices with the cold syrup. Seal, label, and freeze.

Canning. Choose firm, tart apples. Pare, core, and cut the apples into quarters or halves. To keep from darkening, place the apples in a solution of 2 tablespoons of salt and 2 tablespoons of vinegar per gallon of water. Soak no longer than 20 minutes.

Drain and rinse the apples before boiling for 5 minutes in apple juice, water, or a thin sugar syrup. (To make about 5 cups of a thin syrup, combine 2 cups of sugar with 4 cups of water and cook until the sugar dissolves.) Allow 1-1½ cups of liquid for each quart of fruit. Pack the apples into clean, hot, quart canning jars to ½ inch of the top; cover with boiling syrup, juice, or water leaving ½ inch headspace. Seal. Process for 20 minutes in a boiling water bath. Approximately 3 pounds of apples will yield 1 quart.

Fruit yields:
3 medium-size apples = 1 pound
1 medium-size apple = 1 cup peeled, cored, and chopped
3 pounds apples = 1 quart canned halves
1 pound apples = 1 pint frozen slices

<u>Recommended</u> <u>uses</u> <u>for</u> <u>favorite</u> <u>varieties:</u>

Cortland: snacks, salads, pies, sauce, baking

Empire: snacks, salads, sauce, pies

Golden Delicious: snacks, salads, pies, baking

Granny Smith: snacks, salads, pies

Jonathan: snacks, pies, sauce, freezing

McIntosh: snacks, salads, pies, sauce, baking

Northern Spy: snacks, salads, sauce

Red Delicious: snacks, salads

Rome Beauty: snacks, pies, sauce, baking, freezing

Stayman: snacks, baking, freezing

Winesap: snacks, baking, freezing

York Imperial: pies, baking

Old-Fashioned Apple Pie

Pastry dough for 9-inch, 2-crust pie

1 cup white sugar

2 teaspoons all-purpose flour

$\frac{1}{4}$ teaspoon nutmeg

$\frac{1}{2}$ teaspoon cinnamon

6-8 large apples, peeled and sliced

2 tablespoons butter or margarine

1 egg white, slightly beaten (optional)

Roll out half the dough to form a bottom crust and place in a 9-inch pie pan. Mix together the sugar, flour, nutmeg, and cinnamon; rub a little of the sugar mixture into the pastry. Arrange the sliced apples in overlapping circles in the pastry. Sprinkle with remaining sugar mixture; dot with the butter. Roll out the remaining pastry; place on top of the apples; press the edges together; trim. Flute the edges; cut slits in the top. Brush with the egg white. Bake in a preheated 400°F oven for 40-45 minutes. Remove to a wire rack; cool. Serves 6-8.

Sour Cream Apple Pie

Crust: 1⅓ cups all-purpose flour

⅛ ½ teaspoon salt

1 teaspoon cinnamon

½ cup shortening

4-5 tablespoons apple juice or water.

Combine the flour, salt, and cinnamon in a large bowl. Using a fork or pastry blender, cut in the shortening until the mixture is crumbly. Sprinkle in enough juice to moisten the dough. Gather into a ball. Roll out on a lightly floured surface to form a 12-inch circle. Fit the dough into a 10-inch pie pan. Turn under any excess pastry flush to the rim; flute the edges.

Filling: 1 egg

1½ cups sour cream

1 cup white sugar

¼ cup all-purpose flour

2 teaspoons vanilla extract

6-8 large apples, peeled and sliced

Beat together the egg, sour cream, sugar,

flour, and vanilla until smooth. Stir in the
apples. Spoon the filling into the prepared
pie shell. Bake in a preheated 450°F oven for
10 minutes; reduce the heat to 350°F and
bake for 35 minutes. Meanwhile prepare
the topping.

Topping: $\frac{1}{2}$ cup butter or margarine, softened
$\frac{1}{2}$ cup all-purpose flour
$\frac{1}{3}$ cup white sugar
$\frac{1}{3}$ cup firmly packed brown sugar
3 teaspoons cinnamon
1 cup chopped walnuts

Combine the topping ingredients in a small
bowl; mix well. Remove the pie from the oven;
sprinkle the topping evenly over the filling.
Return the pie to the oven and bake at
350°F for 15 minutes or until the topping
is lightly browned. Remove to a wire rack;
cool. Serves 6-8.

11

Wagon Wheel Apple Pie

Crust: 2 cups all-purpose flour
$\frac{1}{2}$ teaspoon salt
$\frac{2}{3}$ cup shortening
2 tablespoons butter
1 cup shredded American cheese
4 tablespoons water

In a large bowl, combine the flour and salt. Cut in the shortening and butter until the dough is pea size. Add the cheese. Sprinkle with the water; blend lightly with a fork. Gather into a ball. Roll out half of the dough and fit into a 9-inch pie pan to make the bottom crust.

Filling: $\frac{1}{2}$ cup raisins
$\frac{1}{2}$ cup chopped nuts
$\frac{2}{3}$ cup firmly packed brown sugar
1 tablespoon all-purpose flour
1 teaspoon cinnamon
$\frac{1}{2}$ teaspoon grated lemon rind
6 large apples, peeled and sliced
2 tablespoons lemon juice

1 tablespoon butter
Milk

Combine the raisins and nuts; set aside.
Combine the brown sugar, flour, cinnamon,
and lemon rind; set aside. Arrange half the
apples in the pie shell; sprinkle with half the
raisin mixture and half the sugar mixture.
Repeat the layers; sprinkle with lemon juice;
dot with butter.

Roll the remaining pastry to form a 6×12-inch
rectangle. Cut into 12 one-inch-wide strips.
Arrange the strips on the pie like spokes on a
wheel, meeting in the center. Twist each strip
and attach to the pastry edge; flute the edge.
Brush the strips with milk. Bake in a preheated
400°F oven for 30-45 minutes. Cover the pie
with foil if the crust browns before the
apples are tender. Remove to a wire rack;
cool. Serves 6-8.

Apple-Mince Pie

3 medium-size apples, peeled and sliced

3 tablespoons all-purpose flour

2 tablespoons butter or margarine, melted

9-inch unbaked pie shell

2 cups mincemeat pie filling

$\frac{1}{2}$ cup all-purpose flour

$\frac{1}{4}$ cup firmly packed brown sugar

1 teaspoon cinnamon

$\frac{1}{3}$ cup butter or margarine

$\frac{1}{4}$ cup chopped walnuts or pecans

Mix the apples with 3 tablespoons flour and 2 tablespoons melted butter. Place in the pie shell. Top with the mincemeat filling. Mix $\frac{1}{2}$ cup flour, the brown sugar, cinnamon, and $\frac{1}{3}$ cup butter until crumbly; stir in the nuts. Sprinkle evenly over the mincemeat. Bake in a preheated 450°F oven for 10 minutes; reduce the heat to 350°F and bake for 25-30 minutes. Remove to a wire rack; cool slightly before serving. Serves 8.

Maple Apple Pie

6-8 large apples, peeled and sliced
9-inch unbaked pie shell
2 eggs, beaten
1 cup maple syrup
$\frac{1}{3}$ cup rolled oats
$\frac{1}{3}$ cup shredded coconut
1$\frac{1}{2}$ tablespoons butter, melted
$\frac{1}{2}$ teaspoon vanilla extract
$\frac{1}{4}$ cup chopped nuts
$\frac{1}{2}$ teaspoon cinnamon

Place the sliced apples in the pie shell.
Mix the remaining ingredients; pour over
the apples. Bake in a preheated 350°F
oven for 1 hour. Remove to a wire rack;
cool. Serves 6-8.

Serve warm with a scoop of maple
walnut ice cream.

German Apple Cake

6 medium-size apples, peeled and thinly sliced

¼ cup white sugar

2 teaspoons cinnamon

3 cups all-purpose flour

1½ cups white sugar

4 eggs

1 cup cooking oil

2 teaspoons vanilla extract

⅓ cup orange juice

1½ teaspoons baking soda

1½ teaspoons baking powder

* Confectioners' Sugar Glaze

Toss the apple slices with ¼ cup sugar and the cinnamon; set aside. Mix together the flour, 1½ cups sugar, eggs, oil, vanilla, orange juice, baking soda, and baking powder. Beat with an electric mixer at medium speed. (The batter will be very thick.) Spread a third of the batter in a greased 10-inch tube or bundt pan; top with half of the apple mixture. Repeat the layers, ending with batter. Bake in a preheated 350°F oven for

16

1 hour. Remove the pan to a wire rack; cool for 10 minutes. Remove the cake from the pan. Cool completely before drizzling Confectioners' Sugar Glaze over the top. Serves 12-16.

* <u>Confectioners' Sugar Glaze</u> : Beat together 1½ cups confectioners' sugar, 2 tablespoons softened butter, 1½ teaspoons vanilla extract, and 1-2 tablespoons water until smooth.

Jane's Apple Crunch Cake

1 cup cooking oil

2 eggs

1 cup white sugar

2 cups all-purpose flour

1 teaspoon salt

$\frac{1}{2}$ teaspoon nutmeg

1 teaspoon cinnamon

1 teaspoon baking soda

5 apples, peeled and chopped

1 cup chopped nuts

1 teaspoon vanilla extract

$\frac{1}{3}$ cup brandy (optional)

In a large bowl, beat together the oil, eggs, and sugar. Add the flour, salt, nutmeg, cinnamon, and baking soda; mix well. Stir in the apples, nuts, vanilla, and brandy. (The batter will be very stiff.) Spread the batter in a greased 9x13-inch pan. Bake in a preheated 350°F oven for 35-45 minutes. Remove the pan to a wire rack; cool. Serves 10-12.

Serve with a dollop of whipped cream.

18

Two-Layer Apple Party Cake

3 cups all-purpose flour

2 cups white sugar

1 cup mayonnaise

$\frac{1}{3}$ cup milk

2 eggs

2 teaspoons baking soda

$1\frac{1}{2}$ teaspoons cinnamon

$\frac{1}{2}$ teaspoon each: nutmeg and ground cloves

5 medium-size apples, peeled and chopped

1 cup raisins

$\frac{1}{2}$ cup chopped nuts

1 cup heavy cream, whipped

Using an electric mixer set at low speed, beat together the flour, sugar, mayonnaise, milk, eggs, baking soda, cinnamon, nutmeg, and cloves for 2 minutes. (The batter will be very thick.) Stir in the apples, raisins, and nuts. Spoon into 2 greased 9-inch cake pans. Bake in a preheated 350°F oven for 45 minutes. Remove to wire racks; cool for 10 minutes. Remove the cake from the pans; cool completely. Fill and frost with whipped cream. Store in the refrigerator. Serves 12-16.

19

Sour Cream Apple Cake

$\frac{1}{2}$ cup butter or margarine, softened

1 cup firmly packed brown sugar

$\frac{1}{2}$ cup white sugar

1 cup sour cream

1 egg

2 cups all-purpose flour

1 teaspoon cinnamon

1 teaspoon baking soda

$\frac{1}{2}$ teaspoon salt

3 medium-size apples, peeled and chopped

1 cup chopped nuts

Confectioners' sugar

In a large bowl, cream together the butter, brown sugar, and white sugar. Mix in the sour cream and egg. Add the flour, cinnamon, baking soda, and salt; mix well. Fold in the apples and nuts. Pour into a greased 8-inch square pan. Bake in a preheated 350°F oven for 25-30 minutes. Remove to a wire rack; cool slightly in the pan. Sprinkle with confectioners' sugar. Serve warm. Serves 6.

Apple Coffeecake

2 cups all-purpose flour

¼ cup white sugar

2 teaspoons baking powder

¼ cup butter or margarine

1 egg

⅔ cup milk

3 medium-size apples, peeled and thinly sliced

½ cup firmly packed brown sugar

½ teaspoon cinnamon

¼ teaspoon nutmeg

⅓ cup butter, melted

Combine the flour, white sugar, and baking powder. Cut in ¼ cup butter with a fork until the mixture is crumbly. Add the egg and milk; mix just to combine. Pour into a greased 9-inch round pan. Arrange the apple slices evenly around the top. Combine the brown sugar, cinnamon, and nutmeg. Sprinkle over the apples; drizzle with the melted butter. Bake in a preheated 375°F oven for 25 minutes. Remove to a wire rack; cool slightly in the pan. Serve warm. Serves 8.

Apple Torte

Crust: ½ cup butter or margarine, softened
$\frac{1}{3}$ cup white sugar
1 cup all-purpose flour
½ teaspoon vanilla extract

Cream together the butter and sugar; add the flour and vanilla. Mix well. Pat into the bottom of a greased 10-inch springform pan. Refrigerate.

Filling: 1 (8-ounce) package cream cheese, softened
¼ cup white sugar
1 egg
½ teaspoon vanilla extract
5-6 medium-size apples, peeled and sliced
$\frac{1}{3}$ cup white sugar
½ teaspoon cinnamon
¼ cup chopped walnuts (optional)   TOP

Combine the cream cheese, ¼ cup sugar, the egg, and vanilla; beat until smooth. Spread over the chilled crust. Toss the apples with $\frac{1}{3}$ cup sugar and cinnamon to coat. Arrange the apples in concentric circles over the cream cheese.

22

mixture. Sprinkle with the nuts. Bake in a pre-heated 400°F oven for 10 minutes; reduce the heat to 375°F. Bake for 20-25 minutes, until the apples are tender. Remove the pan to a wire rack; cool for 25 minutes before detaching the sides of the pan. Serves 8-10.

Apple Crisp

1 cup rolled oats
1 cup all-purpose flour
1 cup firmly packed brown sugar
1 cup white sugar
1 cup butter or margarine
1 teaspoon cinnamon
$\frac{1}{2}$ teaspoon nutmeg
6-8 large apples, peeled and sliced

Combine the oats, flour, sugars, butter, cinnamon, and nutmeg; blend together until crumbly. Place the apple slices in a greased 9x13-inch pan; top with the oat mixture. Bake in a preheated 350°F oven for 40 minutes. Serve warm or cold. Serves 10.

Crispy Baked Apple Dessert

6 medium-size apples, peeled and sliced

$\frac{1}{2}$ cup white sugar

$\frac{1}{2}$ teaspoon cinnamon

$\frac{1}{4}$ teaspoon nutmeg

$\frac{1}{2}$ cup maple syrup

3 tablespoons water

2 tablespoons butter, melted

$\frac{1}{3}$ cup shortening

$1\frac{1}{4}$ cups all-purpose flour

3 tablespoons milk

3 tablespoons butter, melted

Mix the apples, sugar, cinnamon, and nutmeg; place in an ungreased 2-quart baking dish. Mix the syrup, water, and 2 tablespoons butter; pour over the apples. Using a pastry blender or fork, cut the shortening into the flour until the mixture is crumbly. Add the milk; mix until the flour is moistened; form into a ball. On a lightly floured board, roll out the dough to fit the top of the baking dish. Place over the apples; brush with 3 tablespoons melted butter. Bake in a preheated 350°F oven for 30 minutes; remove from the oven. With a sharp knife, cut the crust into small pieces, mixing the pieces into the apple filling. Return to the oven and bake until the apples are tender and pieces of crust are golden, about 30 minutes. Serve warm. Serves 6.

Serve warm with cream.

Apple Foldovers

1 package pie crust mix

½ cup plain yogurt

¾ cup cider

3 tablespoons honey

3 large apples, peeled and chopped

¼ cup raisins

1 tablespoon lemon juice

1 teaspoon grated lemon rind

2 teaspoons cornstarch

¼ teaspoon cinnamon

2 tablespoons cider

2 tablespoons butter, melted

Stir together the pie crust mix and yogurt until blended. Form into a ball, cover, and chill. In a large skillet, combine ¾ cup cider and the honey. Bring to a boil, stirring to dissolve the honey. Add the apples, raisins, lemon juice, and rind. Simmer, uncovered, for 5-8 minutes, stirring occasionally. Mix together the cornstarch, cinnamon, and 2 tablespoons cider; stir until smooth; add to apple mixture. Stir and cook until thick, about 5 minutes. Cool.

Divide the chilled dough into 6 balls. On a floured board, roll each portion to form a 6-inch circle. Brush with the melted butter. Place 2 tablespoons of apple filling on half of each circle. Fold the pastry over the filling; seal the edges by pressing with a fork. Place the foldovers on an ungreased baking sheet. Cut slits in top crust of each. Bake in a preheated 400°F oven for 15 minutes, until lightly browned. Serves 6.

Serve warm with a dollop of sour cream.

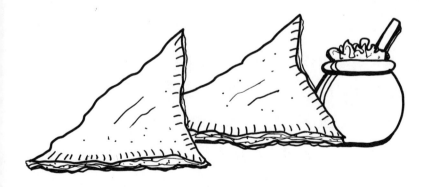

Apple Dumplings

1 package active dry yeast
½ cup warm water
⅓ cup butter, melted
2 tablespoons honey
1 teaspoon salt
1 egg
2 cups all-purpose flour
¼ cup honey
¼ cup chopped nuts
¼ cup raisins
1 teaspoon cinnamon
8 apples, peeled and cored
Butter

In a large bowl, dissolve the yeast in the warm water. Add ⅓ cup melted butter, 2 tablespoons honey, and the salt; beat in the egg. Add the flour and mix well to form a soft dough. Roll out the dough on a lightly floured board to a 12×24-inch rectangle. Cut into eight 6-inch squares. Mix together ¼ cup honey, the nuts, raisins and cinnamon. Fill each apple with this mixture; dot with butter. Place an apple in the center of each square of dough. Moisten the edges of the dough with water, bring the corners together, and seal at the top. Place on a greased baking sheet. Cover; let rise in a warm place for 45 minutes. Bake in a preheated 350°F oven for 1 hour. Serve immediately. Serves 8.

To glaze the dumplings, combine 2 cups confectioners' sugar with enough milk to moisten. Spoon over the hot dumplings.

Johnny Appleseed Bars

1 cup all-purpose flour
½ teaspoon salt
½ teaspoon baking soda
1 teaspoon cinnamon
1½ cups rolled oats
⅔ cup firmly packed brown sugar
½ cup shortening, melted
1 egg
1 teaspoon vanilla extract
½ cup chopped nuts
3 large apples, peeled and thinly sliced
Confectioners' sugar

In a large bowl, combine the flour, salt, baking soda, and cinnamon. Add the oats, brown sugar, shortening, egg, and vanilla; beat until smooth. Press half the dough into the bottom of a greased 9-inch square pan. Sprinkle evenly with the nuts. Arrange the apple slices over the nuts.

Roll the remaining dough between 2 sheets of waxed paper to form a 9-inch square. Remove the top sheet of waxed paper; place the dough over the filling; remove the bottom paper. Press lightly around edges. Bake in a preheated 350°F oven for 25-30 minutes. Remove the pan to a wire rack; cool; sprinkle with confectioners' sugar. Cut into 18 bars.

Honey-Baked Apples

6 large apples
6 tablespoons honey
$\frac{1}{4}$ cup firmly packed brown sugar
Cinnamon
Nutmeg

Core the apples, being careful not to cut the whole way through. Peel about one-third of the way down the stem end. Combine the honey and brown sugar; pour into the center of each apple. Sprinkle each with cinnamon and nutmeg. Set the apples in a large baking dish; pour 1 inch of hot water in the bottom of the dish. Bake in a preheated 350°F oven for 45-50 minutes. Serves 6.

Apple Fritters

2 eggs, separated
$\frac{1}{2}$ cup honey
1 cup plain yogurt
2 cups all-purpose flour
$\frac{1}{2}$ teaspoon nutmeg
$\frac{1}{2}$ teaspoon salt
$\frac{1}{2}$ teaspoon baking soda
1 tablespoon butter, melted
4 medium-size apples
Oil for frying

Beat the egg yolks with the honey until smooth; blend in the yogurt; set aside. Combine the flour, nutmeg, salt, and baking soda; add to egg mixture. Stir in the melted butter. Beat the egg whites until stiff; fold into the batter. Peel and core the apples. Slice horizontally into $\frac{1}{4}$-inch rings.

In a deep fryer or heavy saucepan, pour in enough oil to measure $\frac{3}{4}$ inch deep. Heat to 370°F. Dip the apple rings into the batter; coat thoroughly. Deep fry 3 or 4 at a time in the hot oil, turning once to brown both sides (about 4 minutes). Until all the apples have been cooked, keep them warm in a 200°F oven in a shallow baking dish lined with paper towels. Makes about 24 fritters.

Serve warm with maple syrup or sift confectioners' sugar over top just before serving.

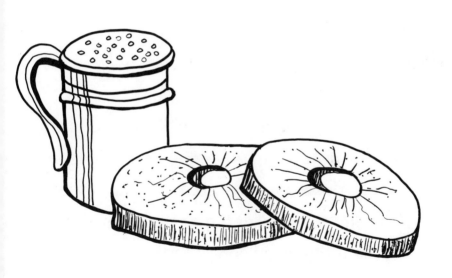

Apple Walnut Cobbler

5 medium-size apples, peeled and sliced

½ cup white sugar

½ teaspoon cinnamon

½ cup chopped walnuts

1 cup all-purpose flour

½ cup white sugar

1 teaspoon baking powder

¼ teaspoon salt

1 egg, beaten

½ cup evaporated milk

⅓ cup butter or margarine, melted

¼ cup chopped walnuts

Place the apples in a greased 9-inch round cake pan. Combine ½ cup sugar, the cinnamon, and ½ cup nuts. Sprinkle over the apples. Combine the flour, ½ cup sugar, the baking powder, and salt. In a separate bowl, beat together the egg, milk, and butter. Add to the flour mixture; mix until smooth. Pour over the apples; top with ¼ cup nuts. Bake in a preheated 350°F oven for 40-50 minutes, until the top is golden brown. Serve warm. Serves 6-8.

34

Barb's Easy Apple Bread

1⅓ cups all-purpose flour
¾ teaspoon baking soda
½ teaspoon salt
1 teaspoon cinnamon
¼ teaspoon cloves
1 cup sugar
½ cup cooking oil
2 eggs, beaten
1 teaspoon vanilla
2-3 apples, peeled and coarsely chopped
½ cup raisins
½ cup chopped nuts

Combine the flour, baking soda, salt, cinnamon, and cloves. In a separate bowl, mix together the sugar and oil. Add the eggs and vanilla; beat well. Stir in the apples, raisins, and nuts. Add the dry ingredients; mix well. Turn into a greased 9x5x3-inch loaf pan. Bake in a preheated 350°F oven for 1 hour. Remove to a wire rack; cool for 10 minutes. Remove the loaf from the pan; cool completely. Makes 1 loaf.

35

Apple Quick Bread

¾ cup white sugar

⅓ cup butter or margarine, softened

1 egg

2 cups all-purpose flour

1 teaspoon baking powder

½ teaspoon baking soda

⅓ cup orange juice

2 apples, peeled and chopped

¾ cup raisins

½ cup chopped nuts

Cream together the sugar and butter. Add the egg; beat well. In a separate bowl, combine the flour, baking powder, and baking soda. Add alternately with the orange juice to the egg mixture. Mix until just moistened. Stir in the apples, raisins, and nuts. Turn into a greased 9x5x3-inch loaf pan. Bake in a preheated 350°F oven for 1 hour. Remove to a wire rack; cool for 10 minutes. Remove the loaf from the pan; cool completely before serving. Makes 1 loaf.

Apple-Oatmeal Bread

1½ cups all-purpose flour

1 teaspoon baking powder

1 teaspoon baking soda

1 teaspoon salt

1 teaspoon cinnamon

½ teaspoon nutmeg

⅔ cup firmly packed brown sugar

1 cup rolled oats

1 cup coarsely chopped walnuts

2 eggs

¼ cup milk

¼ cup butter or margarine, melted

2 medium-size apples, coarsely shredded

Combine the flour, baking powder, baking soda, salt, cinnamon, and nutmeg. Stir in the brown sugar, oats, and nuts. In a separate bowl, beat the eggs, milk, and butter until well mixed. Add all at once to oatmeal mixture. Add the apples and stir just until the liquid is absorbed. Spoon into a greased 9x5x3-inch loaf pan. Bake in a preheated 350°F oven for 1 hour. Remove to a wire rack; cool for 10 minutes. Remove the bread from the pan; cool completely. Makes 1 loaf.

Whole Wheat Apple Bread

2 cups all-purpose flour
2 cups whole wheat flour
2 packages active dry yeast
$\frac{1}{2}$ cup warm water
1 cup milk
3 tablespoons honey
1 egg, beaten
1 cup raisins
2 apples, peeled and chopped
1 egg yolk
1 teaspoon milk

Combine the all-purpose and whole wheat flours; set aside. Dissolve the yeast in the warm water; set aside. In a small saucepan, scald 1 cup milk. Add the honey; cool. In a large bowl, slowly pour the milk mixture over the beaten egg. Add the dissolved yeast. Stir in the raisins,

38

apples, and 3 cups of the combined flour. Knead
in the remaining flour.

Place the dough in a greased bowl, turning
to grease the top. Cover; let rise in a warm
place until doubled in bulk, about 1 hour. Punch
down; form a loaf. Place in a greased
9x5x3-inch loaf pan. Cover; let rise in a
warm place until doubled, about 45 minutes.
Beat the egg yolk with 1 teaspoon milk
and brush on top of the loaf.

Bake in a preheated 375°F oven for 45-50
minutes. Remove the bread from the pan
and cool on a wire rack. Makes 1 loaf.

For a hearty snack, top a slice of bread
with cheddar cheese and place under
the broiler until the cheese is melted.

Apple Breakfast Buns

2 ½ cups all-purpose flour

4 teaspoons baking powder

½ teaspoon salt

¼ cup butter or margarine

¾ cup milk

2 tablespoons butter, softened

4-5 apples, peeled and chopped

½ cup chopped nuts

½ cup raisins

2 tablespoons white sugar

¼ teaspoon cinnamon

¼ cup maple syrup

In a large bowl, combine the flour, baking powder, and salt. Using a pastry blender or fork, cut in ¼ cup butter until the mixture is crumbly. Mix with milk to form a moderately stiff dough. Knead a few times. Roll out to form a large, ¼ inch thick rectangle. Spread with 2 tablespoons butter. Combine the apples, nuts, raisins, sugar, cinnamon, and maple syrup; spread evenly over the dough. Starting at the long edge, roll the dough like a jelly roll; press the edges to seal. Cut into 1-inch slices; place cut side up, 1 inch apart, on a greased baking sheet. Bake in a preheated 375°F oven for 30 minutes. Serve warm. Makes 10-12 buns.

Drizzle with Confectioners' Sugar Glaze (page 17) if desired.

Maple Walnut Apple Muffins

2 cups all-purpose flour
4 teaspoons baking powder
1 teaspoon cinnamon
$\frac{1}{4}$ teaspoon nutmeg
$\frac{3}{4}$ cup milk
1 egg, slightly beaten
$\frac{1}{3}$ cup shortening, melted
$\frac{1}{3}$ cup maple syrup
2 medium-size apples, peeled and chopped
12 walnut halves

Mix together the flour, baking powder, cinnamon, and nutmeg. In a separate bowl, combine the milk, egg, shortening, and syrup; add to the flour mixture. Stir until just moist. Stir in the chopped apples. Fill greased muffin cups about two-thirds full. Top each with a walnut half. Bake in a preheated 400°F oven for 20-25 minutes. Remove muffins from pan and cool on a wire rack. Makes 12 muffins.

Serve warm with whipped cream cheese.

Caramel Apples

1 pound vanilla caramels
2 tablespoons water
6 medium-size apples
Chopped walnuts or peanuts

Combine the caramels and water in the top of a double boiler. Cook, stirring constantly, until the caramels are melted and smooth. Stick a wooden skewer into the blossom end of each apple. Dip each apple into the caramel syrup, turning to coat completely. Immediately roll half of the apple in the chopped nuts. Place on a waxed paper-covered cookie sheet. Chill until the coating is firm. Serves 6.

Cinnamon Apple Rings

6 medium-size apples, peeled and cored
1 cup white sugar
2 teaspoons cinnamon
$\frac{1}{2}$ cup cider
1$\frac{1}{2}$ cups water

Slice the apples horizontally into $\frac{1}{4}$-inch rings. In a large saucepan, combine the sugar, cinnamon, cider, and water. Cook until the sugar is dissolved. Drop the apple slices into the syrup. Cook on low to medium heat for 1 hour, turning the rings frequently. Serve warm or cold. Serves 6.

A festive side dish to serve with roast pork, spareribs, or pork chops.

44

Apple Butter

1 gallon apple cider
4 pounds apples, cored, peeled, and quartered
2 cups white sugar
1 teaspoon cinnamon
1 teaspoon ginger
$\frac{1}{2}$ teaspoon ground cloves

Heat the cider to boiling in a large saucepan or Dutch oven. Boil uncovered until the cider is reduced to 2 quarts, about $1\frac{1}{4}$ hours. Add the apples; heat to boiling. Reduce the heat and simmer uncovered, stirring frequently, until the apples are soft, about 1 hour. (If a smooth butter is desired, press the apples through a sieve or food mill at this point.) Stir in the sugar, cinnamon, ginger, and cloves; heat to boiling. Reduce the heat and simmer uncovered, stirring frequently, until no liquid separates from the pulp, about 2 hours. Heat to boiling. Pour into hot, sterilized canning jars, leaving $\frac{1}{4}$ inch head space; seal. Process for 10 minutes in a boiling water bath. Makes about $3\frac{1}{2}$ pints.

45

Applesauce

2½ pounds apples
Water
½ cup white sugar
¼ teaspoon cinnamon

Peel and core the apples; cut into quarters. Place in a large saucepan and cover with water. Bring to a boil, reduce the heat, and simmer for 10 minutes. Crush the apples thoroughly with a potato masher. Add the sugar and cinnamon. Simmer for 15-20 minutes longer. Pour into plastic freezer containers; cool. Freeze or store in the refrigerator. Makes about 1 quart.

Variations: combine with 1 cup pureed apricots or raspberries. Combine with 1 cup crushed pineapple and 1 teaspoon ginger. Combine with 2 cups cranberry sauce.